To my dear family: Pops, Mom, Pervis, Cleedi, and Yvonne Staples —M.S.

To all who lift their voices in protest and praise —C.B.W.

To the music makers in my life —S.W.

ROCKY POND BOOKS
An imprint of Penguin Random House LLC, New York

First published in the United States of America by Rocky Pond Books,
an imprint of Penguin Random House LLC, 2024

Library of Congress Cataloging-in-Publication Data is available.

ISBN 9780593624692
1 3 5 7 9 10 8 6 4 2
Manufactured in China · TOPL

Design by Sylvia Bi · Text set in Gumbo · The illustrations were created digitally in Procreate and Photoshop.

BRIDGES INSTEAD OF WALLS
THE STORY OF MAVIS STAPLES

by **MAVIS STAPLES** and **CAROLE BOSTON WEATHERFORD**

illustrated by **STEFFI WALTHALL**

 Rocky Pond Books

I'LL TAKE YOU THERE

THERE is Mound Bayou, Mississippi,
where the Staples family sharecropped
and sowed their deep faith.
Where a teenage Roebuck Staples sang
in the church choir and played blues guitar

into the wee hours at juke joints.
Never mind that his devout family
frowned on the so-called "devil's music."

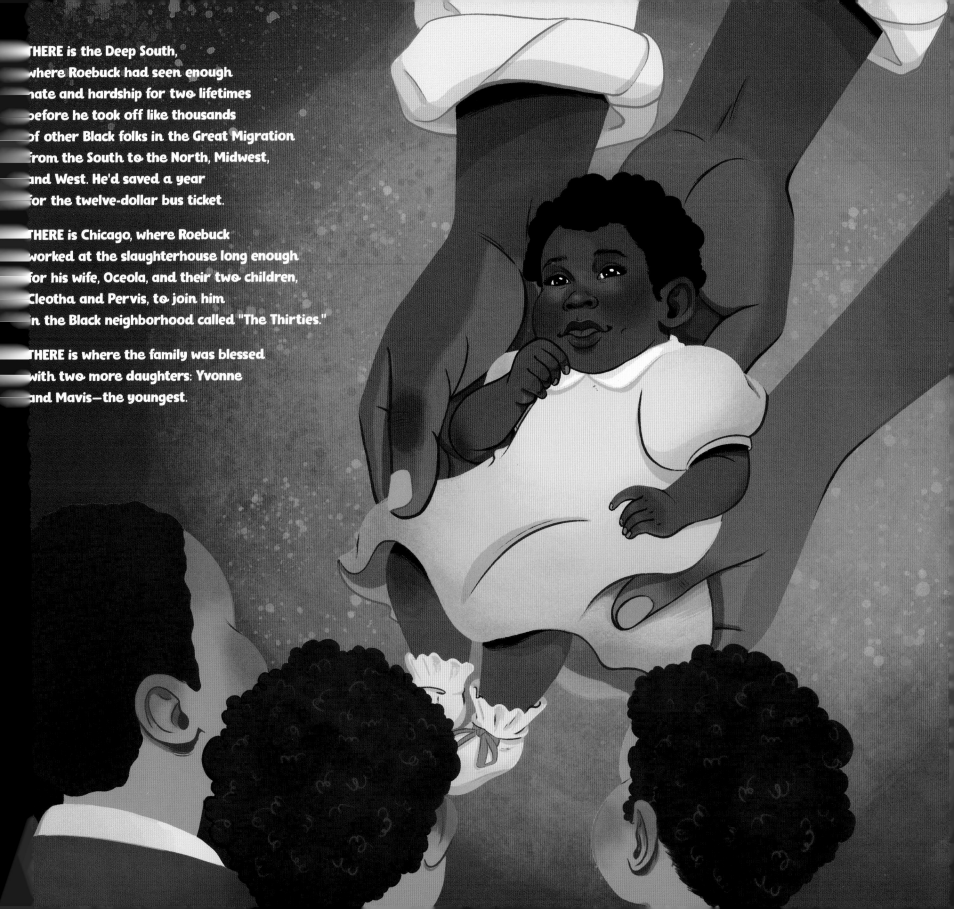

THERE is the Deep South,
where Roebuck had seen enough
hate and hardship for two lifetimes
before he took off like thousands
of other Black folks in the Great Migration
from the South to the North, Midwest,
and West. He'd saved a year
for the twelve-dollar bus ticket.

THERE is Chicago, where Roebuck
worked at the slaughterhouse long enough
for his wife, Oceola, and their two children,
Cleotha and Pervis, to join him
in the Black neighborhood called "The Thirties."

THERE is where the family was blessed
with two more daughters: Yvonne
and Mavis—the youngest.

THIS LITTLE LIGHT

When Black people moved up North
the blues came with them,
humming on assembly lines,
in steel mills, and on construction sites,
where Pops Staples worked to give
his loved ones a better life.
Saturday mornings, he treated the children
to a movie. And Saturday nights,
he made popcorn balls and peanut brittle.
Sundays were for church.
The older children sang in the choir.
But Mavis was still too young.
Mama dressed Mavis and Yvonne like twins.
The sisters slept together, Yvonne
sucking her thumb and twirling Mavis's hair.
Outdoors, Mavis played hopscotch
and hide-and-seek, jumped double Dutch,
climbed fences, and spun on the ice
in secondhand skates.

Pops had told his children,
"Don't start nothin'. . . but don't take nothin' either."
Mavis did just that:
She stuck up for Yvonne against bullies.
"Don't worry," she told Yvonne.
"No one's going to mess with you anymore."

The Staples family knew how to have fun,
but they were firmly rooted in their faith.
Card-playing and secular music were banned.
Progressive Baptist Church was their rock.
With the choir so lively,
how could Mavis not jump up and clap?

DOWN IN MISSISSIPPI

Mighty hard to keep four kids in brand-new shoes.
Not enough cash for four pairs of brand-new shoes.
So, the kids sent South to Grandma's dared not refuse.

Grandma taught the young ones who they were and whose.
She preached the gospel truth of who they were and whose.
There was good and bad and children had to choose.

"Since I Fell for You." Little Mavis sang those blues.
Teenage Uncle Ham caught her belting out the blues.
He couldn't wait to get home to tell Grandma the news.

She made Mavis fetch a switch; then gave her a whipping.
Grandma warned against the blues as she gave her that whipping.
Mavis wrote her parents: Save me from Mississippi.

No one ever told Mavis what songs she could sing.
No one ever told Mavis what songs not to sing.
All she knew was that she'd heard honest-to-God swing.

IF I COULD HEAR MY MOTHER PRAY AGAIN

With Pervis, Cleotha, Yvonne, and Mavis gathered around,
Pops plucked his seven-dollar pawn-shop guitar
and assigned vocals for four-part harmony.
Pint-sized Mavis, then just seven years old,
was a baritone even back then.
She had a voice deep as a valley
and a temper hotter than a volcano.

Led by Pops, the four siblings practiced,
but stubborn little Mavis was slow to learn
the tunes. Somehow, Aunt Katie,
who lived with the family, taught her to sing
"If I Could Hear My Mother Pray Again."
In time, the group's harmonizing was so good
that Aunt Katie invited them to sing at her church,
where Pops's brother Chester was the pastor.
Along with Pops and Pervis, the sisters—
in off-white quilted skirts and blue blouses
that Aunt Katie bought for them—
rode the streetcar to Holy Trinity Baptist Church.

Standing on a chair to reach the mic,
a bashful Mavis stared at the ceiling
rather than meeting the audience's gaze.
The quintet sang the only two songs
they'd practiced.
After the crowd begged for an encore,
Pops figured they'd better learn more songs—
in a hurry. They'd been invited to perform
at another church the next Sunday.

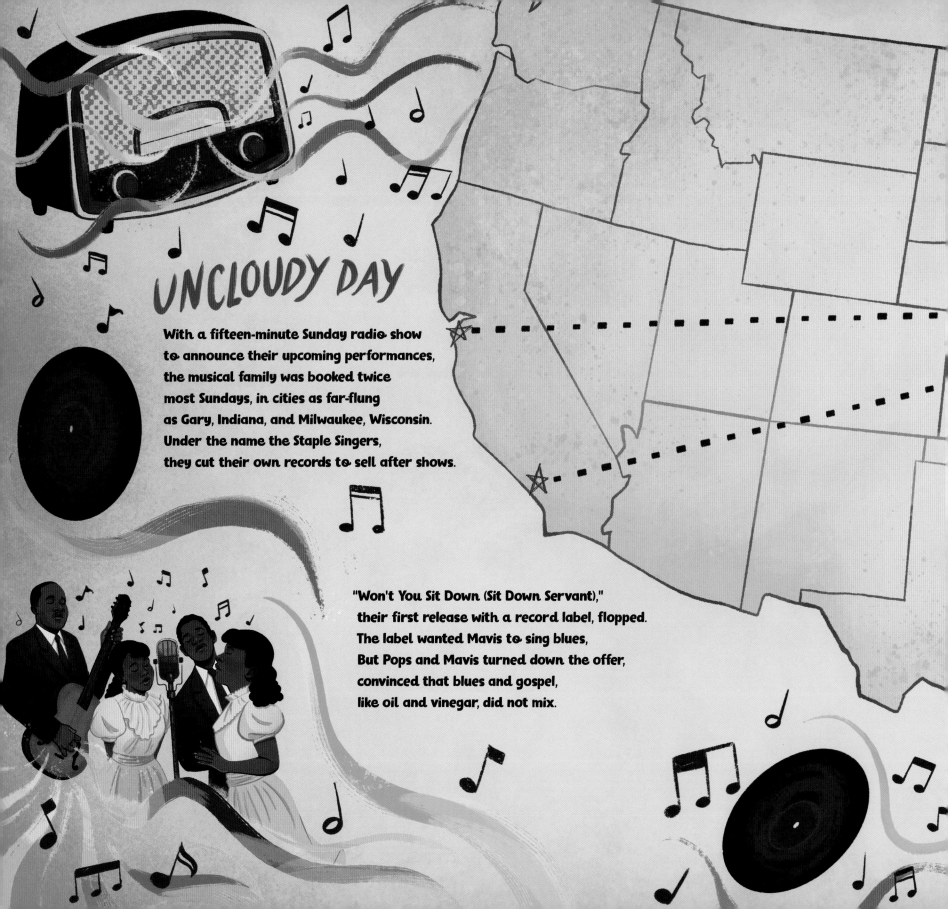

UNCLOUDY DAY

With a fifteen-minute Sunday radio show
to announce their upcoming performances,
the musical family was booked twice
most Sundays, in cities as far-flung
as Gary, Indiana, and Milwaukee, Wisconsin.
Under the name the Staple Singers,
they cut their own records to sell after shows.

"Won't You Sit Down (Sit Down Servant),"
their first release with a record label, flopped.
The label wanted Mavis to sing blues,
But Pops and Mavis turned down the offer,
convinced that blues and gospel,
like oil and vinegar, did not mix.

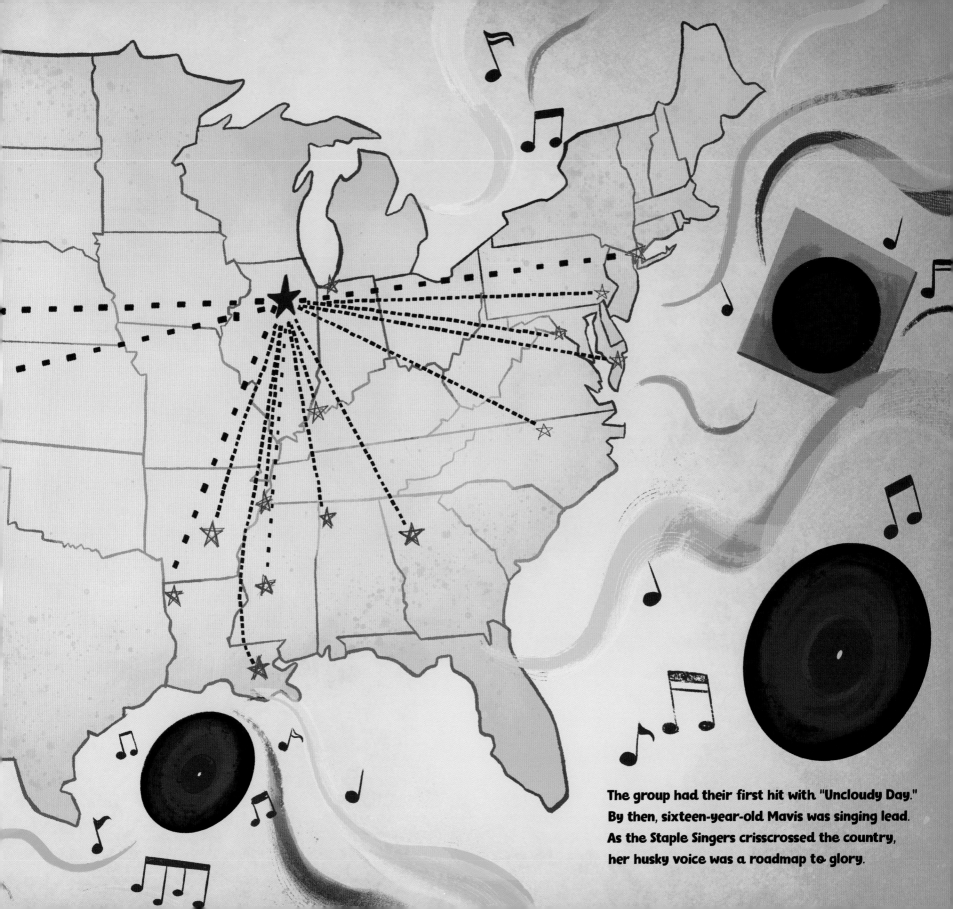

The group had their first hit with "Uncloudy Day."
By then, sixteen-year-old Mavis was singing lead.
As the Staple Singers crisscrossed the country,
her husky voice was a roadmap to glory.

NOBODY CAN MAKE IT ON THEIR OWN

Nobody can make it on their own.
Not without the granite cornerstone of community,
the loving foundation of family,
the window of lofty visions,
and bronze pillars of living inspiration
to shelter dreams from the chill of doubt.

For Mavis, the cornerstone was the South Side—
home to scores of Black churches
and hundreds of thousands of newcomers,
among them blues musicians with names
as vibrant as their lyrics: Muddy Waters,
Howlin' Wolf, Big Bill Broonzy,
Shaky Jake Harris, Lefty Dizz,
Koko Taylor, and Washboard Sam.

For Mavis, the foundation
was Pops's electric guitar trembling
in a blues key, and his firm hand and heart
gluing family harmonies together in praise.

For Mavis, the window was the one framing
a windblown Lena Horne as she crooned
"Stormy Weather" in the film of the same name.
To Mavis, Horne was more than a pioneer—
the first African American actor to land
a contract with a major Hollywood studio;
she was the prettiest woman in the world.
When Pops introduced Mavis to Miss Horne,
the teenage fan was speechless.
Lena returned the admiration.

For Mavis, the pillar was Mahalia Jackson,
who reigned over gospel's golden age.
Mavis was playing with her dolls when she first
heard Jackson's majestic contralto.
Upon learning that the Staples family
would open for the Queen of Gospel,
Mavis sang all around the house.
Her mother warned her
not to get on Jackson's nerves.
Mavis approached the singer anyhow:
"Hello, Miss Sister Mahalia Jackson."

Jackson replied, "I want to hear you sing."
"You'll hear me," said Mavis.
"I sing real loud." Then, Mavis grabbed
her jump rope to head outside.
That's when Sister Mahalia stopped her.
"Don't run outside in damp clothes,"
she said, "if you want your voice to last."

SWING DOWN, CHARIOT (LET ME RIDE)

As word spread about the Staple Singers,
the crowds grew until the foursome
was performing not only in churches
but also in large auditoriums packed
with thousands of gospel music fans.
The Staples liked to make audiences
think that Pervis was about to do a bass solo,
then, right on cue, Mavis would sing instead.
She soon overcame her initial shyness
and couldn't wait to go out and sing.

APOLLO

APOLLO

STAPLE SINGERS
SOUL STIRRERS &
DIXIE HUMMINGBIRDS

The Staple Singers Live!

Off they'd go in Pops's new Cadillac—
once driving two thousand miles from Chicago
to Los Angeles without stopping at a hotel.
Usually three shows per destination:
morning, afternoon, and evening.
They shared the bill with the Soul Stirrers,
Dixie Hummingbirds, and others,
and sold records during intermission.
In Memphis, rocker Elvis Presley
came to their show wearing a motorcycle jacket.
"I like the way your daddy plays that nervous guitar,"
Elvis told Mavis. She had no idea who he was.

THE BACK ROAD INTO TOWN

In the segregated South, the family was barred from whites-only hotels and restaurants. So, they ate homemade sandwiches and slept at Black boardinghouses or motels or in their car.

THE NEGRO MOTORIST GREEN-BOOK

The good-looking Black family
in the green Fleetwood Cadillac had brushes
with white drivers who tried to run them off the road
and with police who pulled them over without cause.
Seeking safety in numbers, gospel groups
sometimes traveled in caravans.

In Mississippi, Mavis refused
to try on shoes after a shopkeeper
told her to use a separate fitting room.
Not even fame could shield the Staple Singers
from racial discrimination.

USE WHAT YOU GOT

From ages nine to eighteen,
Mavis was a part-time student,
touring with homework in her suitcase,
learning lessons along the way.
She would grow into her purpose
and the power of her instrument.

But little Mavis didn't understand
why crying audience members pressed
money into her hands after she sang.
"Those are happy tears,"
her mother explained.
"They're releasing burdens."

When she graduated from high school,
Mavis wanted to be a nurse.
Pops told Mavis, "You're already a nurse.
When you sing, you're healing people."
He had his own prescription for the Staple Singers:
to hit the road full-time.

FREEDOM HIGHWAY

Pops had admired Dr. Martin Luther King Jr. ever since hearing
him on the radio in the 1950s.
So, Pops arranged a sit-down with the young pastor.
After service at Dexter Avenue Baptist Church,
the civil rights leader and gospel performer
put their heads together. Dr. King considered music
vital to the civil rights movement.
And Pops declared, "If he can preach it,
we can sing it." With that, the Staple Singers
headed in a bold new direction:
message music reflecting the headlines
and Black hopes.

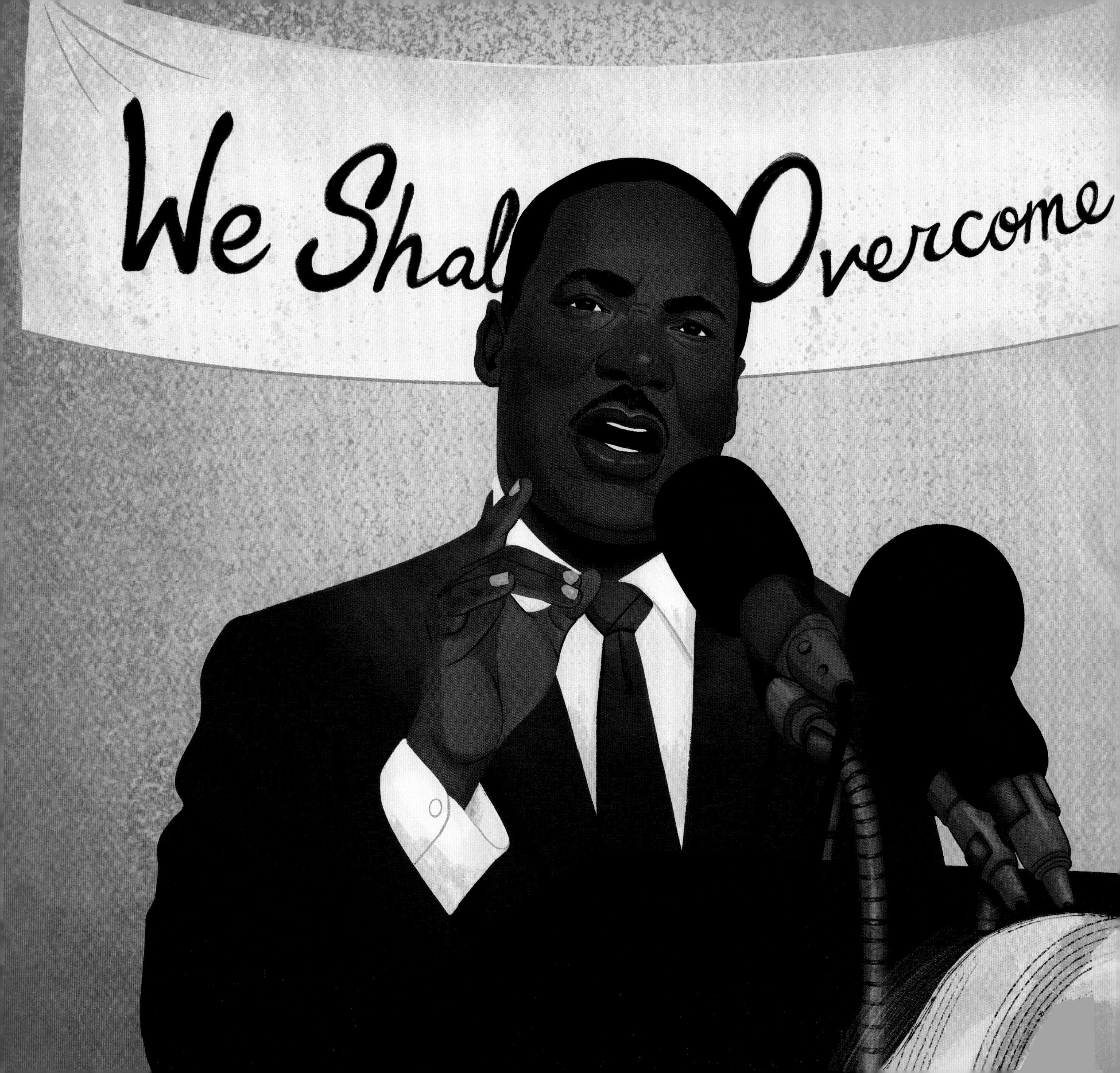
We Shal
Overcome

With new purpose, Pops penned songs
and sought songwriters whose lyrics
spoke to pressing issues of the day.
"Freedom Highway" after police attacked
voting rights protesters in Selma, Alabama.
"Long Walk to D.C." to commemorate
the 1963 March on Washington.
"When Will I Be Paid" to chronicle
past injustices African Americans have endured
and the need for reparations.
"Why? (Am I Treated So Bad)"
for the Little Rock Nine, Black students
who'd sought to integrate
a whites-only high school.

The Staple Singers opened rallies
for Dr. King, rousing audiences
with song before he spoke.
Their harmonies were the soundtrack
of the movement for change.

I GOT TO BE MYSELF

With a voice as deep as a river
and as dusky as the night,
Mavis attracted offers
of brighter spotlights, larger stages,
and fatter paychecks.
Producers tried to tempt her:
Sing secular music.
Launch a solo career.
Leave Chicago.

Devoted to her family and to her faith,
Mavis was in no hurry to take the leap.
In time, she would sing rhythm and blues
and would record as a solo artist—
when Pops and the Lord said so.

But she never moved from her hometown.

LET'S DO IT AGAIN

By the time Hollywood came calling,
the Staple Singers had already crossed over
from gospel and message music to soul.
Sidney Poitier, the first Black actor to win
an Academy Award, was set to direct
Let's Do It Again, an action-comedy film.
The movie had an all-star Black cast and a score
by hitmaker Curtis Mayfield, a Chicago friend
who brought the Staple Singers on board.
Wary of turning off gospel music fans,
Pops at first turned down the offer,
saying, "I'm not gonna sing that.
I'm a church man."

But Mavis and her sisters—eager to hear
themselves in a movie—changed Pops's mind.
And the sultry soundtrack album was a hit—
the Staple Singers' only number one album.

BRIDGES INSTEAD OF WALLS

For Mavis and her family, music was a bridge.
A bridge from the South to the South Side,
where the kids mingled
with budding crooners like Lou Rawls and Sam Cooke.
A bridge from the Baptist church to Carnegie Hall.
A bridge between gospel and folk music
that forged a bond between Mavis and Bob Dylan.
A bridge from gospel to message music,
from segregation to civil rights.
A bridge from message music to soul,
a bridge from Freedom Summer to Summer of Soul,
a Harlem concert series that attracted thousands.
A bridge that carried a skinny, knock-kneed girl
from Chicago's Dirty Thirties to the world:
Europe, Africa, Australia, and Asia.
The Staples family sang African chants
and recorded a Japanese folk song.
For Mavis, music was a bridge.

TOP OF THE MOUNTAIN

When Mavis met Elvis,
A.K.A. the King of Rock and Roll,
he was a teen heartthrob who had fallen
under the spell of gospel as a boy.

When Mavis met Dr. King,
the civil rights leader rarely smiled.
But when he laughed,
joy shook the room.

When Mavis met Prince,
the multi-talented musician,
she kissed him on one cheek.
He bid her to kiss the other too.

When Mavis sang at the inauguration
of President John Kennedy in 1961,
she did not dream of later singing in the White House
for Barack Obama, the first Black president.

When you have sung for a Prince,
two kings, and two presidents,
and befriended queens of soul and gospel,
what mountain is left to climb?

I WILL TRUST IN THE LORD

One by one, members of the Staple Singers sang their last refrains, took their last bows. First Pops, then Cleotha, then Yvonne—whom Mavis had never traveled without—and then Pervis . . . until the only voice remaining was Mavis's, tinged with loss, but still a powerhouse.

She pondered memories
and poured her sorrow
into solo efforts, even funding
one album herself with credit cards.
That's how hard she believed.
Her solo albums bear out
the source of her strength.
Have a Little Faith.
One True Vine.
You Are Not Alone.

YOU GOT TO EARN IT

Between Mavis and the Staple Singers,
they won five Grammys and more
for lifetime achievement.
Had two number-one hits:
"I'll Take You There"
and "Let's Do It Again."

Gold albums and one platinum.
A Kennedy Center Honor and induction
into the Rock & Roll Hall of Fame.
Dubbed "God's Greatest Hitmakers."
And Mavis herself named among
the 100 Greatest Women of Rock and Roll.

As perhaps the highest compliment,
she heard her golden oldies
sampled by new generations—
hip-hop artists like Ice Cube,
Whodini, Big Daddy Kane, and more.
Rap lyrics and the Staples's hits;
an unbroken circle of song,
with Mavis's mighty contralto
soaring above it all.

WHODINI

HOZIER

JON
BATISTE

KANE

BIG
DADDY KANE

ICE CUBE

RESPECT YOURSELF

The Gospel according to Mavis:

Family is the strongest unit in the world.
Love your sisters and brothers.

Don't put anyone down.
Look at everyone the same.

Love comes in all colors.
Give love to someone you don't know.

Believe in yourself.
Know that nobody's any better than you.

Put your heart in anything you do.
Keep the faith.

I'm the messenger.
I just can't give up
while the struggle's still alive.
We've got more work to do.

RECOMMENDED LISTENING

Uncloudy Day, The Staple Singers (Vee-Jay, 1959)

Freedom Highway, The Staple Singers (Epic, 1965)

Mavis Staples, Mavis Staples (Stax/Volt, 1969)

Be Altitude: Respect Yourself, The Staple Singers (Stax, 1972)

Let's Do It Again, The Staple Singers (Curtom, 1975)

Have a Little Faith, Mavis Staples (Alligator, 2004)

You Are Not Alone, Mavis Staples (ANTI-, 2010)

We Get By, Mavis Staples (ANTI-, 2019)

RECOMMENDED VIEWING

Soul to Soul documentary film directed by Denis Sanders (1971)

Wattstax documentary film directed by Mel Stuart (1973)

Mavis! documentary film directed by Jessica Edwards (2015)

Summer of Soul documentary film directed by Questlove (2021)

TIMELINE

JULY 10, 1939
Born in Chicago, Illinois

1950
First Staple Singers performance, at
Chicago's Tabernacle Baptist Church

1956
First Staple Singers hit song,
"Uncloudy Day"

1957
High school graduation

JUNE 16, 1969
First solo album, *Mavis Staples*, released

1972
The Staple Singers' first #1 single,
"I'll Take You There"

1999
The Staple Singers inducted into
the Rock & Roll Hall of Fame

2000
Death of Roebuck "Pops" Staples

2005
Grammy Award for Lifetime Achievement
given to the Staple Singers

2006
National Heritage Fellowship from the
National Endowment for the Arts

2010
Grammy Award for Best Americana
album for *You Are Not Alone*

MAY 7, 2011
Honorary doctorate from
Berklee College of Music

2016
Kennedy Center Honor
recipient

2017
Inducted into the Blues
Hall of Fame

2018
The Staple Singers inducted into
the Gospel Music Hall of Fame

2019
"Spirit of Americana" Free Speech Award
from the Americana Music Association